The Scented Pilgrimage

Al-Faatih
Publishing

Published by: Al-Faatih Publishing UK

www.alfaatihpublishing.co.uk

Author: Iqeel Ahmed

Editor: Maria Ahmed

Cover: Hamzah al-Jundi

ISBN: 978-0-9928729-1-5

To my mother

The best of companions on the most amazing journey

I'm so glad and blessed that your eyes saw the miracles I saw...

Contents

The Departure

سُبْحَانَ الَّذِيْ سَخَّرَ لَنَا هٰذَا وَمَا كُنَّا لَهُ مُقْرِنِيْنَ.

وَاِنَّا اِلٰى رَبِّنَا لَمُنْقَلِبُوْنَ.

"Glory be to Allāh who brought this (vehicle) under our control, though we were unable to control it. Surely we are going to return to our Lord." (Sûrah az-Zukhruf 43:13)

I made the du'ā for travel as I left the house, and the feeling of ease that followed was amazing. We reached the airport early since mum has a 'thing' about being early for everything - and I mean *everything.* The rest of the family piled into the airport to wave us goodbye as well. My younger brother only ever goes to see people off because he feels it's his God given right to be treated to food and drink at the airport (at everyone else's expense).

We said goodbye to the clan and it wasn't as emotional as it had been when we left home... My nieces didn't quite take it so well. Whilst we were waiting for the departure gate to be announced, I found the time to write out my list of du'ās that people had requested. A brother walked over to us after seeing the Hajj tag on our hand luggage, made du'ā for us, and wished us all the best.

Those who know me are aware that I'm prone to the occasional mishap, and it just so happened that I had one right then.

After making my du'ā list, I was sitting anxiously, watching and waiting for announcements. Suddenly, next to our flight number on the departure flights screen, the numbers 11-15 appeared. *Obviously*, I took 11-15 to be the gate number so I grabbed all the bags and made mum rush to Gate 11. There I was trying to explain to the airport staff that the gate had been announced and even took the bloke to the notice board before I realised it wasn't 'Gate' 11-15 - it was the estimated boarding time. I sat down quietly as if nothing had happened and hoped mum wouldn't ask me about it.

We finally learnt of the gate number and sat in the departure lounge. People came over and began offering us food. Sheer excitement was in the air and infectious smiles began to spread over everyone's faces. The spirit of the whole adventure was finally dawning on us and you could genuinely feel it.

Our seats were right next to the small prayer area on the plane. **Result!**

SCENTED TIP
Definitely do your wudhû' before boarding the plane!

I learnt an important lesson on that plane—don't ever leave home without masah! Trying to wash your feet in those plane sinks is truly best left to contortionists. Just as I was going into the cubicle, a man was coming out. I had to call him back because he had left his false teeth there.

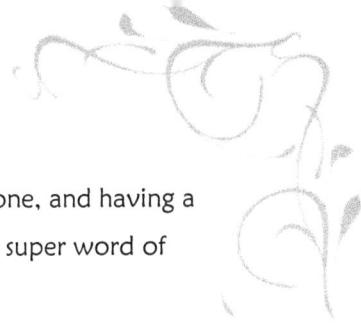

I am so looking forward to being liberated from my phone, and having a break from the hustle and bustle of daily life. In the one super word of William Wallace: *'Freeeeeeedom!!'*

I was waiting to pray in the designated prayer area when a man came up to me and asked me how to put the ihrām garments on. After I showed him, another one came and asked the same question. I asked if they had tried it at home to which they both said no. I wondered... How on earth do you come for this life changing experience and not try on these two pieces of cloth - which if you get wrong - will lead to a moment of embarrassment that you will never, ever forget?!

I was flabbergasted when a third man came over and asked the exact same thing!

SCENTED TIP
Keep some extra safety pins with you - they will definitely come in use for you, or for someone else!

Praying on the plane was strange. I remembered the words of Yûnus ﷺ when he was in the belly of the fish and said, "My Lord! I have adopted a place of worshipping You where no one else has ever worshipped You." He ﷺ had the whole of the depths of the ocean to himself, but I had that little plot high up in the sky. I was a happy man.

The mîqāt was nearing us and the announcement was made. I wanted to be the first to recite the talbiyyah - and I was. *"Labbayk Allāhumma Labbayk"* echoed around the plane. These simple words are like a glue that hold everyone together when recited. Everyone is united by these few words.

Here I am O Allāh! Here I am! You Alone made this possible.

You know my mother's wish and You Alone made it come true.

Glory be to You, for You call even the insignificant back to Your House!

The Arrival

"The best and the most beloved city on the face of this earth to Allāh, is Makkah." (Bukhāri)

We arrived at night. Mum was crying tears of joy - I have never seen her as excited as I saw her then. The look on her face truly summed up what all of this meant to her. Years and years of making du'ā, crying, thinking it was never going to happen, and then counting down the days over the last six months had come down to this. Finally. Alhamdulillāh.

The plane came to a stop and the doors opened. As soon as we stepped out it was like a huge hairdryer blowing hot air at us. *Instant heat.*

We shuffled into the airport and I noticed it had definitely changed since I was here last. So, *so* much better. Last time I came they had us stay on the bus from the plane to the airport for so long that we missed the whole of Fajr! A bus full of Hujjāj and they didn't consider that perhaps we wanted to pray Fajr! *Complete irony.*

Finally I can stop my, **'Don't use the airport toilet'** warning!

They passed us through the airport checks in no time. Just as we sat down thinking we could rest, they told us to get up and move along again. We passed a part of the airport that was packed with African Hujjāj.

Brothers! If you have never waved and given salām to a room full of African brothers, I strongly recommend you do so if you are ever given the chance! You will make an army of friends in seconds. Beautiful smiles māshā Allāh!

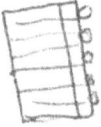

SCENTED TIP

Have some sabr (patience) at the airport. This is part of the test.

If it wasn't for a small hold up at the passport desk because of the group in front trying to wander around the airport, we would have walked right through and out of the airport. The guy that checked our passports called my mum 'Hajji Momma' which made us all laugh.

We got out of the airport and they took us to another waiting area. Our luggage was put into containers and pulled by a buggy - and we followed it. Mum brought my attention to another group of Africans who were having to carry their luggage to the waiting areas and believe me - it wasn't a short distance.

We arrived in the waiting area, relaxed for a while and then prayed our 'Eshā. Mum wanted some water and a beautiful brother overheard her and gave me a bottle.

I made a mental note to remember to make it up to him later.

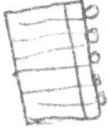

SCENTED TIP

Always show your appreciation to others of the favours they do for you. Remember: *They didn't have to do it.*

We weren't there for long before we were told our coach was ready and so we boarded, handing over our passports as we got on. From the moment we landed to the moment we boarded the coach, it took just under four hours... A new Saudi record me-thinks!

The next salāh will be Fajr at the **Haram!**

We're so close to getting there, what could possibly go wrong now?

The First Sight

"*The best valley on the face of this earth, is the Valley of Ibrahîm.*" (Bukhāri)

All I remembered was sitting on the coach and… that's all I could remember actually. Mum woke me up and told me we had to pray Fajr at this Masjid we had come to. This led me to some serious questions:

1) How did I sleep for 8 hours straight on the coach?
2) Why did it take 8 hours?
3) Where the heck am I?

Mum filled me in and told me that the driver was lost and couldn't find our hotel. I wouldn't normally bat an eyelid but for the tiny fact that we were staying at the Hilton for the first night.. How on earth does a Makkah coach driver not know where the Hilton is?

I clambered out of my seat to make wudhû. The inside of the Masjid was really nice. It had a long back rest that ran along the front row to encourage people to sit in the front and read Qur'ān. *Might have to suggest this for me local back home.*

I suddenly remembered that I had left my phone on the coach. Back home I would have ran to get it, but here I wasn't bothered. *Very strange.*

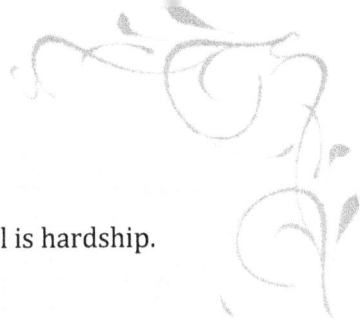

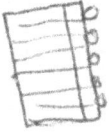

SCENTED TIP

Don't be afraid to rest if you need it. Travel is hardship.

We finally arrived at the Hilton and dropped our bags. I went on a quick little exploring mission and stumbled across a glass elevator, so I decided to take it for a spin. I wanted to check how high it could go and made a plan to take it all the way to the top. I was petrified because I hate heights, but everything is worth a shot here.

I chuckled to myself feeling like Charlie in the glass elevator. As I looked out, I was mesmerised. I saw it in all its' glory... This was what I had been longing to return to. This is what makes you forget everything around you. **The Ka'bah.**

As I looked out, I noticed that there were so few people doing tawāf that it looked like a picture we have on the wall at home... possibly just like every other Asian family.

I forgot all about the escalator plans, and rushed to find mum to tell her that we needed to go right away.

There was a second reason why this trip was so special and that was because my mum has a brother who I last met when I was two years old. He works in Saudi Arabia and was travelling to Makkah to meet us.

We are just minutes away from the meeting. The look on mum's face right now is priceless. Two sights that she has been waiting for, for so long, are soon to be in front of her.

We met him by Gate 1. It was such an emotional meeting for us all.

Mum is very protective over her brother for two reasons. First, she is the eldest sibling and the only sister, and he is the youngest brother. Second, their mother died when my mum was seven years old, and my uncle was a baby. Mum raised him and her two other brothers and dropped out of school to look after the family as their father was very ill too. The sacrifices are unimaginable.

We walked in. Mum kept her eyes closed and held my hand until she was right in front of the Ka'bah.

If I was given nothing in this life but the one ability to continually look at the Ka'bah, that would be more than enough for me.

Here the true reflection of your soul will manifest.

Here is where you will find out so much about yourself.

Here is where it matters.

The First Tawāf

"The space between the Rukn-e-Yamāni and the Hajr-e-Aswad

is a garden from the gardens of Jannah." (Muslim)

I had the tawāf all worked out in my head where mum would stay right behind me holding my hand for all seven circuits. But the problem with plans is.. they rarely go as planned.

It didn't cross my mind that my uncle would be as protective of my mum as I am of her. He took her hand and got stuck into doing tawāf without me. I caught up and stayed at mum's side, protecting her from being carried away by the waves of people, or from following some of the foolishness we see there, such as people rigorously rubbing the Maqām-e-Ibrahîm. (Why oh why?!)

An opening suddenly appeared to touch the Yemeni corner (*Rukn-e-Yamāni*) so I grabbed the opportunity and took my mum with me.

The tawāf was done in no time at all (herein lies the advantage of arriving in Makkah a month before Hajj). We started the sa'î on the mounts of Safā and Marwah and it was completely empty.

The infamous cleaners were out and they splashed water mixed with some sort of cleaning agent over my feet... Quite upsetting considering I was still in ihrām!

We finished, snipped our hair and made our way back to the hotel to change our clothes.

I walked in and found all my roommates in bed - crazy! We were only going to be there for one day before we were to set off for Madînah, so it beat me why they weren't making the most of it! Every moment is precious here.

Mum, uncle and I spent the whole day out. We met amazing people and wondered where on earth that massive green clock came from, along with the lush complex under it.

We met one lady who unfortunately had lost her teenage son the day before during salāh, and had been sitting in the same spot so that perhaps he might find her. They didn't have a hotel and were sleeping outside. She wouldn't even take a cup of tea until my mum forced her.

We spent ages looking for a public call booth but they seemed to have done away with most of them, so we bought sim cards for our phones and tried texting family in England, but no texts seemed to get through either.

I took the sim cards back and the guy told me that due to the amount of people trying to use the networks, they were having real problems with them - which begged the question why he didn't tell me that half an hour ago when I bought them!

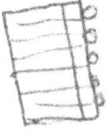

SCENTED TIP

You need your passport when buying a sim card.

Mum was absolutely loving the endless supply of Zam Zam and we were really drinking to our fill.

"The best water on the surface of the earth is that of Zam Zam.

In it there is food for the hungry, and a cure for the ill." (Tabarāni)

I continue to be amazed at how well behaved the youngsters remain at salāh time here. There's no fighting amongst themselves and they always try to get to the front māshā Allāh.

There are lots of stray cats. There are lots of pigeons also. But I like both.

I saw a big group of Hujjāj outside the Haram with their shoulders uncovered. I remembered the hadîth:

"Every act of goodness is charity." (Muslim)

I smiled and corrected them and every single one listened. It is amazing what gentleness can achieve.

SCENTED TIP

If you're going to correct someone, make du'ā for them too.

We went back to the hotel to get our sleeping stuff as I wanted to sleep outside the Haram tonight, as did mum. Let this be a lesson as to how tough we are in Luton! My elderly mum is giving up her comfortable bed in the Hilton to sleep on the hard floor!

In the end, the ladies convinced mum that we had a lot of travelling to do the next day so she would need a good night's sleep, so here I am at 10.55 p.m. sitting with the Ka'bah - a welcomed sight - in front of me, writing as the colourful trains of people pass me by. There is something so hypnotic about it all.

I was faced with a huge issue yesterday and I made du'ā in the Haram for a resolution to it. Not only was it resolved but the resolution was far, far better then I could have ever imagined.

Glory be to you O Allāh! You turned sadness to joy!

My calves are demanding a long shower to make it up with me but I don't think my feet are going to forgive me anytime soon. I think I'm going to be reminded of the pain they've gone through for the next few days.

I'm going to try to bribe them with a nice Radox bath salt soak to try and win

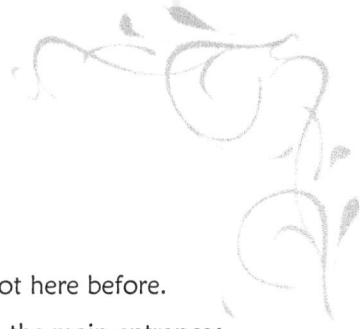

them over...

I noticed some new additions to the Haram that were not here before. They now have see through bags that you can get inside the main entrances for your shoes, and fans that blow air and water at anyone in the vicinity.

I slept outside and got woken twice by the cleaning machines. Nothing makes you jump up like a big machine driving towards your head!

I have a great knack of being able to sleep almost anywhere so that definitely comes in handy here.

I prayed Fajr and made my way back to the hotel. We needed to get our things ready for Madînah.

I'm very chuffed that my bed has not been laid upon once.

The lads in my room want to go for a meal later in the week... I think I'll have steak.

Madînah

"O Allâh! Bestow on Madînah twice the blessings you bestowed on Makkah!" (Muslim)

So we packed our bags, shuffled on to the coaches, and set off for beloved Madînah. Uncle told us he would meet us there.

On the way, mum reminded me about the hijrah and the difficulties that Muslims would have faced - men, women and children, journeying by foot, leaving their home town indefinitely. I could imagine the scenes unfold before my very eyes as I looked out of the window at the empty and uncultivated landscape.

"Verily, those who have believed and those who have emigrated (for Allâh's religion) and
have striven hard in the Way of Allâh, all these hope for Allâh's mercy.
And Allâh is Oft-forgiving, Most Merciful." (Sûrah al-Baqarah 2: 218)

More unimaginable sacrifices.

We've stopped at some service station that looks like the scene from Terminator 2 after the whole area was wiped out. I'm watching a cat. We all throw food for it and I watch it carry a whole piece of chicken in its' mouth without taking a single bite from it.

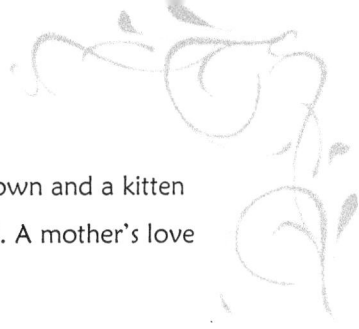

I couldn't work out why until I saw it put the chicken down and a kitten came along and started eating while the cat stood guard. A mother's love is a mother's love.

We're nearing Madînah. It's time to hand over our passports again but the problem is, we have six passports of people who aren't even on our coach, and there are two people on our coach who don't have passports. It looks like we aren't going anywhere fast.

Alhamdulillāh the group sorted the issue out quicker than expected and we were off to our hotel.

We arrived, again at night, and the beauty of Masjid Al-Nabawi was there for all to see. Our hotel is literally next to it.

Mum was over the moon, and it felt good to see her so happy. Feelings of calmness and tranquility sweep right through you in Madînah.

> *"Madînah is like a furnace; it expels out the impurities (bad persons) and selects the good ones, and makes them perfect."* (Bukhāri)

It's a very organised system in this hotel so we were in our rooms in no time. We decided to go to the Masjid right away to give salām to the Messenger of Allāh ﷺ and his two noble companions ﷺ.

I remembered the beautiful du'ā of 'Alî ﷺ:

'Abdullāh ibn 'Abbās ﷺ narrated, "While I was standing amongst the people who

were invoking Allāh for 'Umar ibn al-Khattāb ﷺ who was lying (dead) on his bed,

a man behind me rested his elbows on my shoulder and said,

'(O 'Umar!) May Allāh bestow His Mercy on you. I always hoped that Allāh will keep you with

your two companions, for I often heard Allāh's Messenger ﷺ saying, *I, Abu Bakr and 'Umar*

were (somewhere). I, Abu Bakr and 'Umar did (something). I, Abu Bakr and 'Umar set out.'

So I hoped that Allāh will keep you with both of them.'

I turned back to see that the speaker was 'Alî ibn abi Tālib ﷺ." (Bukhāri)

A brother with us was so overwhelmed that he burst into tears.

We decided to go back and pray in the Rawdha. I had never prayed in there
due to the pushing and shoving that goes on and my fear of accidentally
hurting someone, but I had two old uncles with me who asked me to go with
them so off we went.

It was every bit as packed as I thought. Two huge Turkish brothers were
forming a mini wall allowing people to pray one at a time in a small area. We
took this chance for the two uncles and then the Turkish brothers told me to
pray. It was my first time - and inshā Allāh it won't be my last.

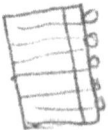

SCENTED TIP
Be patient and don't push even if you are pushed. There are
a lot of testing people out there.

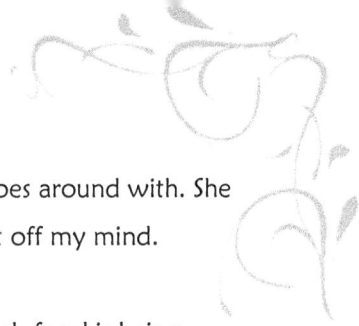

Mum now has a little band of merry women who she goes around with. She tells me not to worry about her now - it's a huge weight off my mind.

We met my uncle after Fajr and ate together. Even though food is being provided as part of our Hajj package, we enjoy eating out. It's another thing that makes me chuckle seeing as mum has never, *ever* wanted to eat out when we were back home.

We did some shopping and it was quite funny how uncle and I both kept competing to keep my mum happy. It's a man thing.

We went back to the hotel so that mum could give her brother the huge bag of clothes she brought over for him along with other bits and bats.

It's amazing to see how he views things. He doesn't look at labels or price, he's just happy with practicality. A beautiful thing.

All the umbrellas are open! Wow, the workers have been busy!

There are umbrellas everywhere and it's a good thing too, as I've never seen so many people in Madînah. I was worried about the crowds in Makkah but this place is **heaving**!

I've never seen women pray outside the designated areas before but there are tons of them so the guards have their hands full ensuring the segregation is to the level we expect in Madînah.

There's a man in my room old enough to be my grandfather. He's a really nice man - truly he is - but he keeps calling me 'Bhai' (which means *brother*). So either he's reliving his youth, or I'm suffering without my Oil of Olay twice a day.

I think I'll have my afternoon siesta outside under an umbrella.

I provided a cup of water for someone, and he was so grateful, yet Allāh provides for the hundreds and thousands of people here each day of their lives.

I don't see a single sad face. Everyone is smiling and happy.

I wonder if there is another place like this in the world.

I was enticed into entering a designer fragrance shop, but a salesman started quoting me £53 for something that would cost me £40 back in England. He couldn't work out why I wouldn't buy it, so when I asked him for a reason as to why I should, he said, 'More barakah in Madînah one!' He looked puzzled as I laughed and laughed my way out of the shop.

A man stopped me and asked for a spare set of clothes but didn't ask me for money. Maybe I am a style icon after all.

More relatives came to see us. I didn't know we had so many here.

I love seeing people who look like people I know - that way I remember the person I do know, and make du'ā for them.

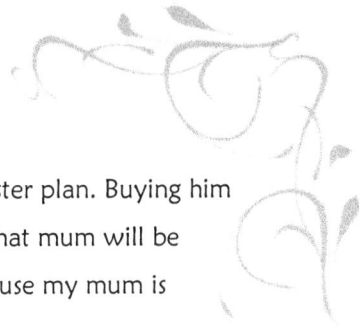

I bought my uncle a watch today. It was part of my master plan. Buying him a present will increase the love between us. On top of that mum will be very happy with me, and that way Allāh is pleased because my mum is pleased...

A simple formula. A watch being a small price to pay for that.

I've got a surprise for mum too (I hope I can pull it off).

I'm not a big fan of shopping before Hajj. I hate thinking about it until I've done the Hajj but because we're going back to England a couple of days after Hajj is complete, I don't have much choice.

At night, a brother and I couldn't sleep, so we grabbed a taxi and went to an area called Sultaania. They have a Next, Dominos Pizza, and so much more...

We sneakily have midnight burgers and swear each other to secrecy from the other lot in the group. No mention is to be made of this dastardly deed.

Madînah Sites - and more

"Madînah is a sanctuary from that place to that.

Its' trees should not be cut and no heresy should be innovated nor any sin should be

committed in it, and whoever innovates in it a heresy or commits sins (bad deeds),

then he will incur the curse of Allāh, the angels, and all the people." (Bukhāri)

It's amazing how you can get two hours sleep and still make it to the Masjid for salāh.

We went to Masjid Qubā' this morning - it was packed! Nothing like the last time I came. I was expecting another Rawdha-like situation but thankfully people were praying and leaving, and making room for others. We travelled there and back for five riyāl in a private van we had hired. What a bargain!

"He who purifies himself at his home and comes to Masjid Qubā' and offers two rak'āts

therein, will be rewarded the reward of an 'Umrah (lesser pilgrimage)." (Ibn Mājah)

Apparently my late night munch buddy didn't go to bed after we returned, and went to the Masjid instead. There he got smacked quite hard by a guard and he's been whining about it all morning and afternoon.

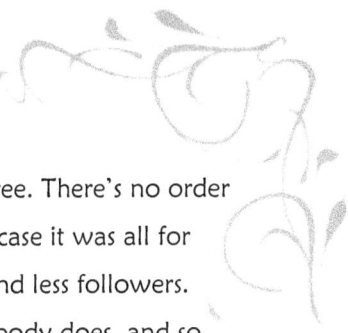

One thing I have learnt is - people go nuts for anything free. There's no order or control with people when it comes to freebies. In this case it was all for a free leaflet or book. This Ummah needs more leaders and less followers. All it would take is for one person to form order but no body does, and so, mayhem ensues.

I arranged mum's treat for the morning. Do not ask me how (because I won't tell) but I arranged for mum to be taken to the Rawdha and to have her own space to pray for as long as she wants without being disturbed.

I too had the same deal and went to the Rawdha. I started making du'ā for everyone I could think of, by their names. I was there for so long that I was even given a chair. Strangers started to shake my hand thinking I was someone of importance! Little did they know...

SCENTED TIP

Make du'ā lists and update them whenever you can - you probably won't remember everything if you don't!

Mum wanted to go shopping. If she saw something that she liked, she would buy it. None of this 'let's keep on looking' window shopping business.

You like it > buy it > take it. Simple. Another reason I love her so much.

A few of the lads decided we were going to go for a midnight tour. We couldn't have picked a more off-key driver... This guy seriously did not like us, and I'm sure he was swearing at us - and it wasn't under his breath either. It

23

was a mad trip. We were having a laugh amongst ourselves and maybe he thought we were laughing at him. Who knows?

We didn't leave on good terms.

We had another midnight munch. We found a different driver to take us back - an amazing guy who knew how to hold great conversation. I was so impressed I actually tipped the guy - and I never tip. He was worth breaking my rule for.

Due to the time restraint we were unable to get mum to the Rawdha at the agreed time. I'm still gutted, but inshā Allāh she will be in there on Friday.

I really have got to stop bringing books with me when I travel here. I always worry I won't find anything here so I bring my own and then end up with five times the amount that I already had.

We got to see the umbrellas close today. *Amazing.*

Me-thinks that starting a conversation with a stranger is becoming a lost art. Many times I started the conversation by offering the man next to me some of my ittr (perfume) and off we went from there. I love it when someone beats me to starting the conversation.

SCENTED TIP

Don't be afraid to meet new people. You will meet the most amazing people - if only you'd let yourself.

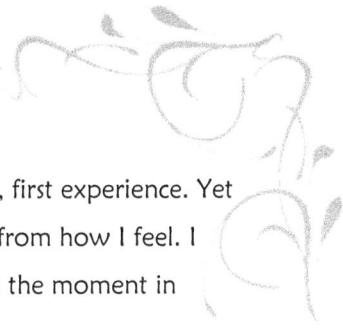

I keep forgetting that for many, this is a once in a lifetime, first experience. Yet somehow I don't think their feelings are all that different from how I feel. I don't think you can ever get relaxed or 'not caught up' in the moment in this sort of environment.

I don't have 'knock in nails' feet like some other men here and my baby soft ones are taking a pounding. So I bought a bucket. I threw in my Radox bath salts, added hot water and soaked my feet. Instant *'aaahhhhhhh'*.

SCENTED TIP

You can learn so much by watching others. It can encourage you to behave in a certain way - or to prevent it.

I saw a young Bangladeshi who I assumed worked in the Masjid. I watched him giving da'wah to a group of Bangladeshi elders. I didn't understand a word, but I understand adab, and he had it in abundance. It was so plain to see alhamdulillāh. He engaged them in an amazing manner, smiled throughout and let them have their say without cutting in. He asked them questions and answered theirs.

When salāh time came and he had to leave, every single one of the elders got up to hug him. Such was the effect he had on them. You could tell it wasn't just out of courtesy - but sheer love.

"He who does not show mercy to the young and show esteem for our elders is not one of us."

(Abu Dāwûd)

My Saudi sim card finally let me start texting England!

Texting off my T-mobile sim has cost me £40 so far and we've only been here for four days. I need to stop taking 'get-jealous' pictures and sending them to brothers.

Wow, they've got Arab boy scouts! It's the funniest looking thing...

The old uncle in our room is *raw*. He doesn't say much, but when he does I wish I could Twitter it.

Don't you hate saying goodbye to someone and then it turns out they are going the same way as you?

It's a lovely feeling sleeping on the carpets outside the Masjid, waking to the adhān and watching thousands of people come for salāh. It's even nicer when the bloke next to you keeps your space while you go and re-do wudhû.

Isn't it annoying when you're praying and people walk right in front of you as if it's normal? I was praying in a designated prayer area out of the way of everyone else, and one bloke just came and stood there.

'Mate the number 31 doesn't pass here so maybe, just maybe, I might be praying?'

I got me some more amazing time in the Rawdha again. I got to do everything I wanted to do. Nobody pushed me, stood in front of me or rushed me. **Proper sukûn.**

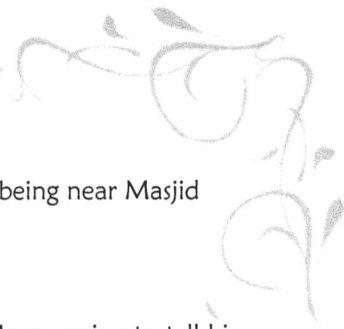

I learnt today that because I kept talking about our hotel being near Masjid 'Alî, my roommates thought that I was a Shî'a!

My mate told me that he gave some street kid 500 riyāl. I was going to tell him to keep his charity to himself until he told me he thought it was 5 riyāl! Apparently the kid was well happy! Well obviously.

Met my first Australian Hajji today. *G'day Mate!* I love eating in back street restaurants. You meet the most interesting people.

Mum was not feeling well but wanted to go on the arranged tour of the sites today. I went on the Urdu coach to be with her. The guy on the tannoy was really laying it on thick. He should have gone into sales.

The coach driver almost crashed into a car, so the car driver got out and tried to go for our driver with a hammer! It eventually amounted to nothing - but road rage was clearly alive in Madînah. I wondered why hammers would conveniently be kept in cars anyway.

We visited the great Mount Uhud. I wondered how much soil has been taken from here over the years as 'souvenirs'. We went to a few other Masājid and visited Masjid Qubā' again.

> "Uhud is a mountain which loves us, and which we love." (Bukhāri)

I still haven't seen any stars since I've been here. It is quite cloudy at night.

I have the official position of tea maker for mum and the ladies in her room. Big responsibility. Word gets around that I make a mean cuppa...

I have a thing where I really don't like eating alone. I'd rather go hungry than eat alone because I find it depressing. This evening I took my food and sat on the pavement just in front of the Masjid. I was so transfixed to the Masjid that for the first time in a very, very long time I was able to eat alone. It was all the company I needed.

These 'pretend-Palestinians' have a tough time. I was with a couple of lads from Swansea and we met one with his wife and kid who claimed they had been robbed. My spider sense told me something wasn't right so I walked off and left Swansea lads to deal with it. It was funny watching them get out of it themselves.

Met another the next day with wife and child in tow. Same story. I wondered how many more I would meet.

SCENTED TIP
Beware of fake sob stories!

Mum bought some sandals for me. Look hard but are soft. Rather like me.

Just got a text from England that little Abu Bakr needs a heart transplant operation and every time this message is forwarded the phone company will

donate 2 pence towards the operation. I wonder...

1. Which phone company?
2. Why would they pick little Abu Bakr?
3. How do they know it's been forwarded?
4. Who comes up with this rubbish?
5. How do people fall for it?

I took a friend to the Rawdha and got him in. To say he was happy was an understatement. Actually, to say he was happy is a huge understatement. I could hear him crying and crying in sujûd.

There is something about sujûd in the Rawdha. Somehow you block everything out and it's all just about you and Allāh.

Slight problem - some guys from our group saw us being taken in and I was sure they were going to have some questions later...

It is amazing to think we have been here for less than a week. The things that we have seen and done in this short time span are weeks worth.

My uncle will be leaving later today to get back to work in Tāif. Inshā Allāh he will be able to make it back to Makkah to be with us. The plan is that he'll stay with us for the entirety of the Hajj.

A small part of me wants to do Hajj alone with mum, but I know him being with us will give mum great peace of mind. I think it stems from me wanting to

The Turkish bloke next to me is amazed by me writing this left-handed. He's been watching me write every word. Either that, or he's amazed by my naff handwriting.

I continue playing my 'people that look like someone I know' game. Except the amazing thing is that twice, it has actually been that person.

Amazing the places in which fate brings you together.

And yet another 'pretend-Palestinian' that has been robbed! He was smiling as he told us his sob story.

Complete Focus

And Hajj (pilgrimage to Makkah) to the House (Ka'bah) is a duty

that mankind owes to Allāh..." (3: 97)

I cannot believe how focused I am on Hajj this time.

Nothing matters but this. I cannot think about my past or my future. The only thing that matters is right here, right now.

I really have no idea how my mum has managed to hit her weight allowance just with presents bought for others. My luggage doesn't even weigh a fraction of that. If this keeps up, I'm going to have to look into sending things by cargo.

I fancy an apple.

A fourth 'pretend-Palestinian' has had his money stolen. Wife and kid right behind. What are the odds?

I paid over £5 for a tin opener!

I cannot find Radox bath salts here and I've looked everywhere. I want to share them with others but mum is my priority.

I fell asleep on the carpet outside the Masjid only to be awoken by four Hujjāj from India old enough to be my great grandfathers. They wanted to know about England and I answered all their questions in return for their du'ā that mine and mum's Hajj is made easy. I really, really enjoyed our chat.

I feel like Uncle Albert whenever the first time Hujjāj ask me about my experiences. I have them spellbound with my heroic deeds and near death tales...

I had a late night munch with one of the Swansea lads who is also my regular partner in crime. Great laugh.

Scented woke up feeling rough today. Sore throat, fever and bunged up. I think today shall be a rest day. My plan is to just go for salāh, and come straight back to the hotel.

I have been mistaken for an Arab, a Turk and a South African so far. Scented is a man for all the people...

It is really scary how slow time goes here. It is the complete opposite of normality, of life in England. Here you think you have done something last week, but really it was yesterday. There is definitely lots of barakah (blessings) in Madînah.

Why, oh why did I pack four pairs of socks? It's boiling here!

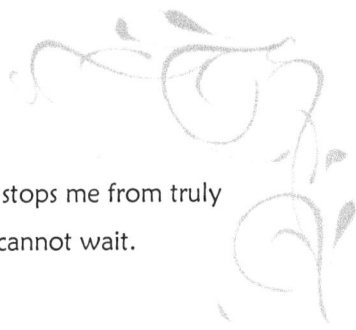

My worry about mum during Hajj is the only thing that stops me from truly looking forward to the huge occasion. Otherwise, I just cannot wait.

You really have got to see their version of boy scouts.

For the first time in my life I saw a bloke praying salāh and then midway look at his watch!

I prayed on the roof of the Masjid today. Beautiful subhān Allāh.

I decided to get myself checked out at the local medical centre. Very quick and very impressive. Beats the NHS…

Huge crickets here! Or are they locusts? Ruddy massive whatever they are.

When I first came here in 2004 our hotel was near a string of food places and there was a man who we used to call 'Pakora wāla' as he seemed to always try to entice us with free pakorai. Lovely guy. We even took photos with him and I still have them.

I saw him today working at a restaurant. He no longer has his shop. He truly looked broken, and it was really sad to see. I told him who I was and how I remembered him but it seemed that they were painful memories for him. Really upsetting to see who he was before, and how unhappy he is now. May Allāh give him the best in this life and the next.

The other day we were in our air conditioned bus and we pulled alongside an old American yellow school bus full of Africans looking tired and hot, many of whom were standing up. Puts things into perspective.

SCENTED TIP
Don't complain about what you don't have, for others have less.

It is an amazing thing walking to salāh not knowing which nationality will be praying next to you. Knowing that for a moment you are going to be standing shoulder to shoulder. You smile at each other, maybe exchange a few words, have a laugh and then stand before the One Lord who has decreed for you to be here and has created you both. Where you stand, all men and women are equal. Allāh alone knows the hearts. **Each heart has its' own story.**

We went to honour an invitation for lunch today. It took me a few minutes to get over how many books the brother we went to see has collected.

We are going to travel to Makkah tomorrow, so we are soon going to go to the Mîqāt to get into our ihrām. Not sure what worries Makkah will hold for mum. The crowds here are worrying enough so who knows what's going to happen there, but Allāh is our Protector and to Him Alone we entrust our affairs.

I watched a little group of kids with no arms begging. After a while they ran over to a woman and she took all their bags of money. She didn't even have the decency to cover up. Miraculously, their arms grew back moments

later.

I take comfort in the punishment for the one who begs without reason. And I don't mean the kids.

Has anyone else noticed the change of air when you get to Bāb as-Salām? It becomes so much cooler. It's as though you cross an invisible barrier.

It was my last night in the Rawdha, except some troublemakers were trying to cause trouble. The guards dealt with them swiftly. For that reason, I was unable to get into the Rawdha itself. It wasn't meant to be but I certainly cannot complain, because I know people would love to have had the opportunities I have had so far.

Mum finally managed to pray in the Rawdha earlier though. She was over the moon and said it was amazing. She's happy - I'm happy.

Swansea lad and I went for a late night hunt for an Internet café. Our lack of Arabic stood against us and he wanted to give up, but I was on a mission again and had to know how this was going to end, so we kept going. We asked and asked for directions until we finally found one.

News! World! So much to check, so little time, and the computer kept crashing. I left happy. *Mission accomplished.*

We Leave for Makkah

"There is no city on earth to which all the prophets, angels, holy messengers, and all the pious servants of Allāh, who reside in the heavens and the earth, including the jinn, flocked to, except Makkah." (al-Muwatta')

We sat in the coach for ages while they loaded up the luggage. The problem with being so close to the Masjid was that the cops kept telling the driver to move on. How's he meant to move, ya'ni?

Our driver seemed like a nice guy. I watched him help people while he waited. Built like a tank. Looked like he could snap your neck in several places for a laugh.

We got told that our coach was going to a separate hotel.

We got to the Mîqāt and put our ihrāms on. Everyone managed to make it back to the coach quickly.

It's finally happening. I cannot make enough du'ā that Allāh makes it easy on us. I ask Allāh to make this the case, by anything I can think of that I have done for His Sake alone.

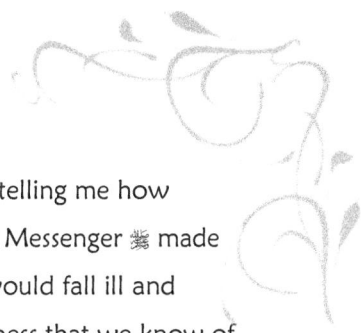

I had an excellent conversation with a Pathãn who was telling me how Madînah was ridden with disease and that when Allãh's Messenger ﷺ made hijrah, the kuffãr in Makkah rejoiced believing that he would fall ill and die. Instead, with him ﷺ came all the blessing and goodness that we know of. He explained it better and it was a joy to listen to.

SCENTED TIP

Think good of others; remember that YOU are a guest of Allãh, before you start complaining

My biggest test so far has been people who complain. These people complain about anything and everything. I cannot stand the constant backbiting and whining. And I cannot stand it when people make stuff up and spread rumours. I really have to bite my hand as the ogre in me feels the need to unleash myself on them.

"...And those who are patient, We will certainly pay them a reward in proportion to the best of what they used to do." (Sûrah an-Nahl 16:96)

It was a long drive and there were few stops. Word reached us that Makkah had had thunder and lightning. I phoned a friend who confirmed it and said that the place was flooded but it was all back to normal now.

The coach was going around in circles which only fueled the gossip mongers

who were convinced that we were going to be dumped miles from the
Haram.

It was 1 a.m. when we reached an underground car park. We got taken to our
rooms and the ladies were next door to us. I supposed that this way I could
keep making tea for them and maintain my ever-so serious responsibility.

There were seven beds on the downstairs floor, and seven on the upstairs
floor. We entered our top floor room and I took the bed by the window. I
pulled back the curtains, and after all the hassle and headache of the travelling -
I was so, *so* overwhelmed that I cannot even begin describing my feelings. We
were overlooking the whole of the Haram! Subhānallāh. This was far more
then I had ever expected.

I sat there for ages just looking out of the window.

Mum wanted to attempt 'Umrah straight away but I was a little worried as Fajr
was around the corner and she would end up alone for salāh.

We reached the Haram and the ground floor was packed, so we made our way
to the first floor. As a rule, I try to avoid the first floor as all the pillars get in
the way and create the bottleneck effect, but mum dislikes heights (as do I) so
we wouldn't tread higher. Given a choice, she would definitely want to keep as
low as possible from the top floor, and the ground floor was way too packed,
so off we went to the bottleneck first floor.

We went around twice and I noticed that the space to walk had already begun

to get enclosed. I could not take the risk of losing mum so I suggested we do the rest after Fajr. I took mum to the back and sat her with some ladies, and I sat at the front but directly in her line of vision so she could see me at all times.

I was so tired and hungry. I was literally fighting to stay awake while we waited for Fajr as I didn't want to redo wudhû and leave mum alone. In my sleepy state, I kept thinking I had to fast.

We prayed Fajr and got back to doing tawāf. It was averaging ten minutes a circuit. It took its' toll on mum and she needed a wheelchair for sa'î.

Many young blokes here are ready to rip people off with rip-off prices for renting a wheelchair. I later learnt that free ones are available if you go early from one of the offices. Some bloke quoted us 300 riyāl and another quoted 200. I found one for 100 riyāl and took it. Mum was relieved and I pushed her myself.

We drank plenty of Zam Zam water and completed the seven rounds.

We finished our 'Umrah, alhamdulillāh, and came out of the Masjid.

Now came the difficult part - finding our hotel! We may have been in the biggest complex in Makkah, we may have had the big green clock on our roof, but for the life of me I couldn't remember where our hotel was...

In my defense, we got dropped there at 3 a.m. and I discovered that the directions we were given were wrong.

We wandered around for ten minutes until we found some guards who directed us after I rang up one of the group leaders to be the middle man on the phone. Another occasion where I wished I knew Arabic.

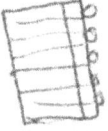

SCENTED TIP

Always keep your hotel details with you!

Mum got a few words in to tell me off but it's all good.

We landed at our hotel, I showered, and I crashed out.

My New Roomies

"Without doubt, the believers are brothers of one another,

so make peace and harmony between your brothers, and have consciousness of Allāh,

so that perhaps He will show you Mercy." (Sûrah al-Hujurāt 49:10)

You may think seven men to a room - all sharing one bathroom - is a bit much, but believe me, there is more than enough room. I've seen one of these brothers around in Madînah and he was always smiling, so I'm happy to have him with me. Another one of them is a serious looking guy who I met a couple of times in Madînah too. The other two are unknown to me. One of them is an elder.

Everyone's getting on fine so far.

Dhuhr was packed.

I met a friend and we had a meal. We had to find a nice spot on the floor to eat on which I found ironic, considering my new hotel. There I was getting moved on by guards as we squatted to eat. Loving it.

I got my bearings of where I was and acted as 'Senior Translator' at the currency exchange for Indian, Pakistani and Bangladeshi families. I must have been good as the Turkish families wanted my services too, but my genius has boundaries so I politely declined!

Thanks to watching way too much television in my irreligious life, every time I get into a lift and nobody is around, I always check to see if the panels above me open - in case I need to do a get-away move. It's useless actually, as my height phobia wouldn't allow me to climb out of anywhere.

I was humming the Mission Impossible theme tune earlier. I was so into it I didn't realise the lift doors opened and people were staring at me. Oops.

I was sitting in my room watching these workmen in the tower next to us. They're pulling the whole building down. I can tell you right now, no amount of money would get me to do what they're doing.

To say that they're risking every single valuable limb on their body is an understatement. *Their lives are at stake!*

I sat looking at the Haram for what seemed like ages.

I feel guilty as many have not and will never see what my eyes are seeing right now. I look and look, and keep looking, as I know I'll kick myself when I leave here for wasting time doing nothing when I could have been enthralled by this amazing sight.

I sat outside all evening, and all night.

My New Roomies

I zoomed to the third floor of the Haram and I probably looked like a right *idiot* grinning from ear to ear running up the stairs. Me and the third floor go way back. It's just as I left it. Few sights on earth are as amazing as watching the thousands of people doing tawāf from the third floor.

You find yourself hypnotised and have no concept of time.

I was sitting downstairs and spent ages just smiling and giving salām to brothers and elders, trying to gain some reward. I remembered the hadîth,

"When you smile to your brother's face, it is charity." (Tirmidhi)

My sinuses are all messed up.

I heard my other uncle is coming from England on the 9th. He may even be with the same Hajj group as us! Exciting times.

Me and Mum

> "Our Lord, forgive me, and my parents and the believers
> on the Day the account will be established." (Sûrah al-Ibrahîm 14: 41)

I saw mum today sitting surrounded by some Indonesian ladies at salāh. When it was time to leave mum embraced them all. It really made me smile.

The group is taking us on a tour of all the sites in Makkah today. I'm not a fan of walking around in the daytime so it's going to be uncomfortable but mum wants to go. The problem with all these places is the large crowds. All it takes is for one person to get lost and we could be here in this *sweltering heat* for ages.

Thankfully the group was very well organised - so nothing happened.

Speaking of the group, I have to say I am completely bowled over by their manner of dealing with us. One chap downstairs fell ill and they took him to the hospital and stayed with him. They check on him every day and tend to anything that needs doing quickly and effectively.

Mum told all the aunties that I got us lost on the way back to the hotel that first morning. One mistake and this is all I'll be remembered for! It'll probably reach the headlines back home.

Mum saw me eating an ice cream and told me I'd get a cough because of it. Ten minutes later I coughed and guess who got an 'I told you so' in? Mum's Curse...

I had a cream cake the size of a subway roll! At first I didn't think I'd make it but I went for its' pressure points and it had to give into my experience and superior technique. It didn't stand a chance.

I went to get my beard trimmed today at a barbers to sort out any split ends and they point blank refused to touch it. I only wanted the split ends removing.

I found out that a new wheelchair costs £52 (320 riyāl), so those who exploit people's weaknesses and needs can charge this amount for leasing one for tawāf and sa'ī, and make their money back in no time.

The amount of times you get smacked at the back of your ankles by people pushing wheelchairs is unreal. These cowboys who rip you off and charge you huge amounts want to get it over and done with as soon as possible so they can go rip someone else off. It's not the fault of the person inside the wheelchair. I'm trying my utmost to take care of myself as mum relies on me. Damage to my feet or legs would make everything so much harder.

I prayed next to an Indonesian brother today. We spoke for ages. He told me that 200,000 Indonesians have come this year and that Hajj is booked out for six years in advance back home. *Wow!*

He had a beautiful little mat to place his head on in sujûd. At the end of the salāh we shook hands and he gave me the mat! I was gutted I didn't have anything to give him. Truly gifts warm the heart, and to give a gift to someone you met just half an hour ago is even more amazing. What a legend māshā Allāh.

I just carried my standard issue Zam Zam water from the designated filling station to the hotel. Ten litres in each hand. Sweating, aching and proper paining - but I made it like Rocky. If anyone loses my water now at the airport, I will beat someone to death with my slipper.

Amazing night. It truly was. It was as if the tawāf was all mine. Huge gaps would appear in the strangest of places. It was done with so much ease yet there were so many people.

My dreams are not making any sense. They're going at 100 mph and contain absolutely everything. I don't think my brain can compute so many experiences happening all at once.

I really hate this new huge clock. I hate anything towering over the Ka'bah. The only benefit of it for me is that it's easy for mum to use as a landmark to find her way back.

The shopping mall under our hotel is a rip off. They have Next, Mothercare, Monsoon and lots of other shops here, but people walk in, see the prices and walk right back out. They're at least twice the price we get them for in England.

Me and Mum

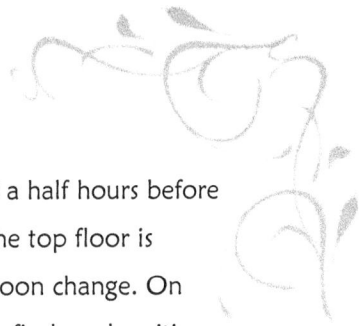

It's Friday and the crowds have come early. It's one and a half hours before salāh, and they've closed the entrances to the Haram. The top floor is empty due to the heat and lack of shade - but that will soon change. On the streets everyone is sitting in whatever shade they can find, and waiting patiently. Some are sitting on the street floor, some on cardboard, others on prayer mats. The fortunate ones get shade next to a pillar or something.

I really cannot believe how relaxed mum is here. It's as if she does this every day. But she doesn't! This truly is doing her the world of good. Now all I have to worry about is how much luggage she's going to try to sneak back into the UK!

I could not have picked a better group for me and mum, and for that, I'm very grateful alhamdulillāh.

Gratitude

"...if you give thanks, I will give you more (of My Blessings)..." (Sûrah al-Ibrahîm 14: 7)

By sheer chance I stumbled onto the fifth level of sa'î. I had never been up there before. It's funny standing on the fifth floor, watching people on the third floor, watching the tawāf. Loads of heads ducking out and looking at the same thing.

One of my roomies came out of the bathroom with his clothes soaked top to bottom with water. Me and the other room-mate from Manchester almost cried with laughter.

I am so grateful for the brothers in our room here. We all look out for each other, help each other and always put the others first. It's a true blessing from Allāh. The last thing you want when you go for such a blessed journey is to have to deal with difficult people sleeping in the same room as you.

SCENTED TIP
Make du'ā for good companions before you embark on this journey. It's so important.

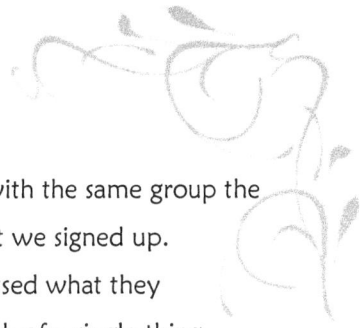

Before I came here, I spoke to brothers who had been with the same group the year before, and it was upon their recommendation that we signed up. They said that after the Hajj they sat together and discussed what they would change if they went again, and they couldn't think of a single thing.

I feel exactly the same. Everything has been far, far more than I could have expected or wished for. The accommodation, the food, the roommates - they're just a few of the countless blessings we have experienced.

I feel like we should have paid a lot more for what we've been given.

I woke up with eyes stinging *real* bad. I guess that's what you get when you rely on two hours sleep before Fajr. I got me a new partner in crime though. *Oh yeah.* Lad from Manchester is up for whatever and whenever.

We spend some quality time in the Haram before we go for a chin wag with the staff at *Bin Dāwūd*. We then attempt to find *Bin Dāwūd* himself as my buddy insists he is a real person, in the same way that Calvin Klein is named after Calvin Klein.

It seems if there are laughs to be had, we're certainly going to have them - but we remind each other also of the favours of Allāh. Alhamdulillāh for companionship. It is as the saying of our predecessor Hasan al-Basri ﷺ,

"*My family reminds me of the dunya and my brothers remind me of the Ākhirah.*"

We find some awesome food places and decide we're going to take all the guys from our floor for a munch. We're also going to sneak sleeping bags into the Haram and kip on the fifth floor of sa'î.

My dreams are getting more detailed now.

I hook Manchester lad up with a Radox bath salt foot soak. I didn't hear a word from him for the next ten minutes. Good way to keep people quiet...

I'm thinking of starting a business by taking my bucket and bath salts to Marwah. It's my biggest Hajj tip to date: Radox Bath Salts.

We have been watching these guys working on the building next to us. What makes a man hang off the side on the fifteenth floor of the building without a safety rope and kick away at the very support he is resting on?

The government should use this as work encouragement: *Get a job or we will send you here!*

It's amazing watching people from up here. At Dhuhr they fill the spaces that are in the shade and then bit by bit as the shade comes across they fill that too.

I was sitting down and an Indonesian brother comes to ask if I'm from Bakersfield, California. I tell him I'm not and he says that there is a bloke in his local Masjid who looks just like me. Seems someone in Bakersfield has been blessed with eye-watering good looks too!

I keep getting free chewing gum with my change in the shops. Are they trying

to tell me something?

I've told mum that from now on she's going to leave her gang of merry women in the evenings, and come with me to sit in front of the Ka'bah.

Today I had just finished praying when I saw a cat pounce on something. I thought cats only did that when they caught a mouse or something like that. I looked closely and it had a pigeon in its mouth. Raar...

I thought that sort of thing only happened in cartoons... It's weird - cats and pigeons are next to each other here all the time. This must be one hungry feline. The cat takes its' dinner and quietly nips into a derelict building. *Wow.*

Amazing. I watch from our window. I can see hundreds of thousands of people and Allāh knows the hearts of each and every single one.

We are so fortunate to have an uncle with us who is a Qur'ān Hāfiz and very wise. I love listening to him. Today we were talking about the achievements of man and how none of them things compare to Allāh's Greatness and Ability. He said something so simple yet so powerful: 'So what if man has stepped on the moon? Allāh took His beloved to the Heavens.'

I will never forget this evening for as long as I live. Me and mum sat on the ground floor right in front of the Ka'bah, just looking at it and making du'ā. I didn't want it to end but mum needed to get back and rest. She asked me to make a special du'ā for myself. She's never asked me to do anything like that before. Bonds are created in the House of Allāh. I am going to bring her every night that we're here inshā Allāh.

Me and Manchester Lad

"Mix with the people on the condition that your Dîn is not jeopardised,
and be jestful with the family." (Bukhāri)

Manchester lad and I went hunting for an Internet café. I remembered seeing one a couple of days ago so we hit the streets. We found it and discovered that they charge 15 riyāl an hour - which was a rip off - but we had no choice. We tried to take in all the news we could. Kind of like, *'quickly eat to your fill before someone takes the food away'* moment. Nom nom nom.

Manchester lad showed me a really good lecture about the Mercy of Allāh. I made a mental note to watch all of it when I got back to England.

I decided to hit tawāf at 2 a.m.

I did, and I loved it.

There was a bit of drama today. I was on my sixth circuit and I accidentally came in between an old Turkish couple. The old man started to shout at me even though I only got between them because I was being pushed and shoved from behind. I put my hands in the air to show him that I wasn't doing anything - and at that exact moment, someone gave me a great, big, *push*.

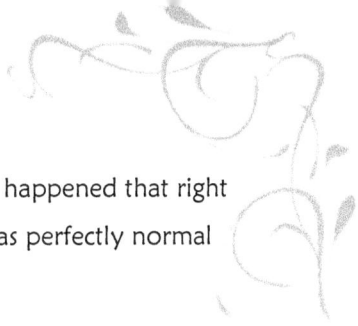

Normally it wouldn't have been a problem but it just so happened that right in the middle of the tawāf, two blokes decided that it was perfectly normal and acceptable to do sujūd there. So I fell over them.

My heroic superpowers came into play and I jumped up as quick as a flash in case I got trampled. That's another one of the annoying things here - well two things - getting trampled, as well as folk praying wherever they please. What's worse is when they choose to pray in the most awkward of places and you interrupt them to advise them, they get upset.

Mum told me that an auntie from her room had her bag stolen from right in front of her while she sat waiting for salāh. It was in a women's only area. The bag was in front of her and a lady came and asked for a bottle of water which was slightly behind her. The auntie turned around and then turned back to give her the bottle. A moment later, she realised the bag was gone. Shameful.

SCENTED TIP

Never keep all your money in one place, and it goes without saying - trust no one with your bags!

Me and Manchester lad acted as elevator attendants today, taking people up and down the floors. We were so good that I reckon if we had kept it up we could have made some serious tips.

Just heard that a Brit from another hotel had lost £2000 during the tawaf. Apparently they took the whole belt.

We were sitting waiting to pray Fajr inside the Haram and saw a group of men arguing with some women who were insisting on sitting right at the front. I understood the fact that they wanted to see the Ka'bah as well, but we have to follow etiquette. This would be like me going and sitting right in the middle of a huge group of women. In the end the ladies got up and went to the back. May Allāh reward them, give them good in this life and the best of the Hereafter.

Just found out that a bloke who I thought was between 20-22 years of age is going to be 40. I can't get over it - I'm gob-smacked.

We insisted on the elder in our group to become the Amîr, and we - Manchester lad, Moshy, Jedda and I - agreed to take any dispute to him to get his verdict. I would be astounded though, if we ended up coming across any matter that needed a decision - such is the harmony and fun we have. Yet me and Manchester lad continue trying to find any little thing just to get a verdict... I want to see a public lashing!

SCENTED TIP
Fun and games with your room mates are so important when you're aware from home - it keeps you sane.

They made the 'prayer for rain' after Fajr today. You don't ever hear *that* living in the UK.

I was on one of my usual 3 a.m. missions when I bumped into a local takeaway owner from my hometown. We've always got on and we met again with big,

manly hugs. He looked so happy to be here.

Just found out the elder in our room (Hāfidh Sāhib) is a father of ten children!

It's pretty amazing what you can get for free as long as you have no shame in asking. This hotel is going to remember me and Manchester lad… It's scary how quickly we formulate plans and the lengths we're willing to go to. The partnership works so well and the opposition do not stand a chance. We come away with many goodies and share them between the others on our floor. I am going to give mine to mum.

When you think about all the crazy practices of the people across the world it's amazing that you don't see any of it here.

Bin Dāwûd are really going to have to stop selling me sweets and chocolates. They're killing my throat.

On the topic of *Bin Dāwûd,* there's a Malaysian worker here who looks really unhappy and clearly doesn't like his job at all. *This guy just would not smile.*

So me and Manchester lad have been working on him every day and now when he sees us he's never without a smile as soon as we walk in. In fact the whole shop sort of lights up… *Oh yeah. My humility is unbelievable.*

But on a serious note, all it takes is a few smiles and a few jokes to change someone's mood.

There was a mobile phone company in the mall under our hotel who were giving out free umbrellas. They ran out but told us that if we came back at 4 a.m. they would give us four umbrellas.

I'm not sure if they doubted us and they probably thought we'd never make it at that time to collect them. It's now 4.15 a.m. and I have *five* umbrellas in my possession. I'm a happy man.

They're trying to serve us sheep hooves for breakfast! Needless to say it's just a cup of tea for me. Some of the others are well happy.

You should see the people when it comes to salāh time, and they have to leave the Black Stone. It takes the guards ages to peel them off it and they keep running back to kiss it. It's amazing. Yet it reminds me of the saying of 'Umar ؓ who approached the Black Stone and said to it,

'By Allāh, I know that you are a stone and can neither benefit nor harm. Had I not seen the

Prophet touching (and kissing) you, I would never have touched (or kissed) you.'

Then he kissed it. (Bukhāri)

They finally restored order for salāh and really, it's surprising that the people are even able to wait for the Imām to give salām before they are back onto it. I only saw it for a brief second after I finished before it was submerged by people all over again.

I was surprised at my DIY skills as I made something (I'm embarrassingly modest so I won't mention it) for Manchester lad. I felt like Bear Grylls saving things to use later. Manchester lad was well happy and I stand proud at my accomplishment.

I keep seeing so many people that look like people I know.

Me and the gang went for a munch. Great laughs took place. Time well spent is time spent in the company of good people. We decided, well I decided to have late night tea. We sat on the ground and just talked and looked at the Haram. Memories like this will last forever.

The lads went to bed and I went into the Haram to sit by the Ka'bah again.

Every time you see it, it feels as if it's the first time.

It's amazing when you see people more than once here. Some you spend just a few minutes with. You meet them, smile at them, joke with them and treat them like your brother. Later on they see you eating, shopping, in the Masjid or just walking - and they come with huge smiles remembering you from the last. It's the Sunnah in full effect.

All the lads are sleeping out tonight. Everyone's making out as though they'll be able to survive on the bare minimum. We shall see.

We went to fill up more containers with Zam Zam water. There were huge queues in the designated filling areas with people trying to take enough to supply a small country! We started using the taps but we ended up having a guard hot on our tails trying to stop us. Manchester lad seemed to be having an easy time so we all flocked to where he was. He started trying to shoo us away.

It's been an amazing night. Sleep was not on the menu tonight. When you look around, you truly see amazing sights before you. Nowhere else in the world will millions of people converge into one place and worship with such purity and devotion. All sit and wait for one man to come and lead them in prayer.

It's tough keeping your spot to pray, especially when you're right at the front. It's funny watching people sneaking around pulling sly ones trying to get to the front.

SCENTED TIP

Share your space with someone else - it doesn't make you any less of a person.

Our roommate Moshy has had breakfast today for the first time in twelve years! Everyone is insisting it goes in my diary, so here it is Moshy, you made history on page 58!

A new roommate joined us today. Everyone made him feel welcome and he fits in so well. I thought he was around 36 years of age but he told me he was close to 50! Either the Makkan air is really agreeing with people or I'm really naff at this game.

Mum called me for something so I went to the hotel and stood outside her

room for a while waiting for her. After a short time I was about to phone her but then I remembered the hadîth in Bukhāri about the man who was trapped in the cave. He made du'ā to Allāh by the deed of standing all night with milk for his parents so as not to disturb them. What an amazing thing. It made me realise how impatient and selfish we are. I stood waiting quietly after that.

Only in Makkah do I get scared by looking up at buildings.

There's no shortage of blokes tapping up every plug socket in the Haram and the shopping centres to charge their mobile phones. Mobiles are like the new-age children.

The best way I can describe people here at salāh time, is that they are like water. They pour into every gap, every space, every opening and every alleyway they can find.

You realise that you're just a tiny ant in this great Ummah.

My slippers have been missing for a whole day. I have to put up with plenty of 'I told you so's' from Manchester lad. I'm going to go later and see if they are still where I left them. We're so close to the Haram that I go to every salāh barefoot. It doesn't even feel strange.

I saw my first dog in Makkah today. It looked so out of place. I also saw a cat on the third floor of the Haram... How on earth did it get up there?

Our new roommate (who we named Cyborg because of his unstoppable quest to fit everything into his day and make the absolute most of his time here) told me that Indonesian and Malaysian couples who are serious about getting married come to Hajj with their families.

This is so that both can see and hear about how the other coped with all the tests and trials that Hajj brings. You really don't know what is going to happen here on a day to day basis, or how you're going to be tested, so it is impossible to keep up an act.

I don't know if it's true for everyone, but I think it's a great idea. A bit expensive, but a great idea.

The Last Addition

"There is no city on earth through which Allāh multiplies one good deed by a hundred thousand, except Makkah." (Bukhāri)

Our roommate Jedda has a unique style of sleeping. He always sleeps on his back and always claims he wasn't sleeping if you mention it.

We have our last addition to the room. He's a very quiet brother who I have seen around before. This is like the perfect room alhamdulillāh. He is given the customary welcome pack from us - bedding, towels and a free umbrella that I picked up from the people giving out telephone sims.

He gets the nickname 'Terminator' because the lads tell me he was fast asleep before he woke up at 2 a.m., said, *'I need to go make tawāf'*, got out of bed in one movement, did wudhū', and was gone.

I went for a late night ice cream and saw a man get his ihrām caught in an escalator. It pulled the garment in and he fell backwards. I jumped into action and held him up, stopping him from cracking his head open.

All in a day's work for Hajji Scented. He was fine, but they didn't have any strawberry sauce for my ice cream.

It's confirmed. I've lost my slippers. They are the first pair I've lost this time I've come for Hajj. I hope they have a good new owner.

I got caught doing 'The Robot' dance in the lift by an Egyptian man. There was no way I was able to explain what I was doing, so I didn't bother.

I found a truly awesome view of the Haram from another room in our hotel which is still under construction. You could see the entire Haram from there, as well as the surrounding areas. I showed the lads. Me-thinks they're going to take their wives and claim that they found it!

All the Hujjāj that were set to do their Hajj this year are finally here now. The Haram is **packed** out. I can't even get a decent view of the Ka'bah from the third floor.

Tomorrow will be the last Jummah before Hajj. This time next week, Hajj will be over. *A scary calculation.*

Nicknames I have been given so far include:

~ Lastminute.com, because of my overly lax attitude.
~ Sherlock, because I love to go investigating.

Oh yes, Manchester lad from this day forth will be dubbed 'Zinger' due to his love of everything big and chicken. Google *'Mighty Zinger'* burger and you will see what I mean.

Zinger tries to educate everyone on what a planetarium is. Apparently it's

where they keep fish!

The story of me and Zinger is quite amazing really. I had bumped into him twice before we shared this room together, and both times I really thought '*I'm not going to get on with this guy*'. Appearances can be so deceiving.

SCENTED TIP

Don't be quick in judging people - you could be *so* wrong.

A person you may think is really good will show their true colours once you share a roof with them. On the flip side, a person like Zinger who I thought I would never in a million years have anything in common with, has become very dear to me. The same thought process applies to everything else around us.

"But perhaps you hate a thing and it is good for you; and perhaps you love a thing and it is bad for you. And Allāh Knows, while you know not." (Sûrah al-Baqarah 2: 216)

Some local lads from back home turned up and wouldn't believe that I'm staying in the Zamzam Towers, so they insisted on coming up to the room. They told me that our bathroom is bigger then their living quarters. For the price they paid and the price we paid I think somehow our reservations got mixed up!

I still hate the clock.

Jummah was jam packed today. The top floor was empty again due to people being unable to sit in the heat for hours on end waiting for the salāh. If you want a spot seeing the Ka'bah, you have to be in there by 9 a.m., and stay there.

I've been showing everyone the view I found. The room has not been completed yet and whoever gets it isn't going to want curtains put in, I promise you that.

I can't believe someone took my slippers again! Awesome slippers they were... Like walking on air. I had to buy some naff ones as all the good ones were sold out. So embarrassing.

We tried flagging a cab down to go and visit Zinger's friends but the drivers were trying to do their level best to rip us off. In the end we gave up.

We will be leaving for Minā tonight, and Makkah is buzzing - far more than usual. People are trying to get all their shopping in. I really wish I had rested more yesterday. I would much rather prefer to leave in the morning but I have mum with me and she wants me to stay with her. My uncle is going to come with the walking group in the morning and meet us in Minā.

Zinger went out and bought a loaf of bread and turkey slices for breakfast in Minā. Ohh ay love! Only Zinger could think of something like that.

I am not allowed to leave the room to go to buy an ice cream until I write that

Terminator has invented mango lassi in Makkah.

Zinger has been trying to buy it but couldn't find it anywhere, and now he's necking it down like it's the last thing on earth and his life depends on it.

Minā - Here We Come

"The pilgrims performing Hajj and 'Umrah are the guests of Allāh; if they call upon Him, He will answer them, and if they ask Him for forgiveness, He will forgive them." (Nasā'i)

We got into ihrām after Maghrib but planned to make our niyyah later. The time for 'Eshā came so we prayed and waited for confirmation for when we would be leaving. We waited and waited. Hours ticked by, and there was still no news. So we nipped out for ice cream with flake.

We had a really good, deep talk regarding how detached we are from real concerns and from those whom are tested more than us. We discussed how helping them is a means for us to help ourselves, and that a measure of a person is to do things for people who cannot benefit us. I told them the story of sister Aafia and her test.

We then broke for Coke and chocolate.

We finally nodded off at around 2.30 a.m. only to be awoken at 4 a.m. to be told the coaches were finally en-route. We had to walk a short distance to where the coaches were going to pick us up.

Fajr was prayed on a dusty road on a little bit of cardboard.

An auntie decided that she wanted a cup of tea so she volunteered me with the task of getting it. I got knocked around by a load of blokes all trying to get their milk and two sugars.

The coaches arrived and some people showed their true colours and completely ignored the women and elderly, and pushed to get on first. I really, really hate it when things like that happen. It is as if the world is going to end and this is the only form of transport that will deliver them to safety. We managed to restore order and we were off.

SCENTED TIP

Wait! Let others on first! You will get a seat!

Me and a revert brother from Swansea got the talbiyyah going in full effect.

The road wasn't as busy as I thought it would be.

We arrived in Minā and got to our tents.

So many people were trying to take up more space than they needed, forgetting that we were still expecting the brothers who were coming on foot.

This is another reason I am so proud of the brothers who roomed with me in Makkah. We just take the space that we need, no more and no less - and when others need space, we make it for them. May Allāh love these brothers. Their hearts are huge.

Zinger whipped out turkey sandwiches and they really went down a treat. Genius, that boy.

As I sit looking around the tent right now, I see different kinds of people. Different because each of them will draw personal experiences from this. Some will use their time well, and others will just complain and backbite. Those who have contentment will have contentment regardless, and those who complain and backbite will do so regardless. I truly make du'ā that I am of the first and Allāh keeps me far from being the second.

The walking group arrived and my uncle was with them. In typical uncle fashion, he refused to sleep indoors for the night. In fact, in Makkah, the brothers in our room kept telling me to get him to stay with us inside our luxury accommodation. But dear uncle wouldn't have it, and preferred the outdoors.

He set his camp up near our tent, and seemed to have this amazing knack of only being a minute away whenever mum or I needed him.

It is *so* annoying when men move the curtain that separates the men and women's tent. They think it's fine as they have someone in there but forget that they're not the mahram's of the other hundred plus.

Uncle found a hospital nearby and stocked up on free medication and other bits which was fantastic as the chemist in Makkah wanted 71 riyāl for a course of antibiotics.

I just saw a Hajji flip because he didn't get a drink with his meal. Proper crazy.

It's gong to be an early night tonight - it's the biggest day of all tomorrow.

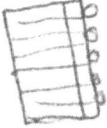

SCENTED TIP

Sleep early before the most important day of Hajj - you will need the energy.

'Arafāt

"There is no day in which Allāh sets free more souls from the Fire of Hell,

than on the day of 'Arafāt..." (Muslim)

We woke up for Fajr and thought it would be ages before the coaches would arrive to take us to 'Arafāt but subhānallāh, the coaches were there and we got to our destination by 9 a.m.

We have water coolers in the tents which we noticed are topped up around three times a day with ice, and we are all given water bottles too. A couple of times I saw some people coming and taking the water bottles out of the container claiming they were topping the containers up. Someone pointed out that these people are the ones camped on the road, and I realised yet again that even here we have something we take for granted, that not everyone has.

'Arafāt is truly amazing. There's something in the air.

You see amazing generosity on 'Arafāt, you see people sleeping the whole day, you see people crying their eyes out, and you see people just wasting time. In short, 'Arafāt is Hajj, because you *will* get what you want from it.

Uncle is a gangster! He prayed inside the Masjid and still tracked us down in our camp. I found out that he has had serious toothache but he's a soldier and has not complained one little bit.

Maghrib came and it was funny watching everyone grab their bags thinking they were going to go to Muzdalifah immediately.

Six hours later our turn arrived and it was worrying how people clambered and ran like they were going to be left behind.

We waited patiently until the very end and got onto the coach. Those who were hasty were by now packed into the coaches like sardines in a tin, but we had loads of room.

Zinger is dishing out cheese on crackers. *I flippin' love him!*

Muzdalifah

"O Allāh! I seek Hajj that is free from ostentation and from seeking reputation" (Ibn Mājah)

Muzdalifah is wide awake at 12:30 a.m.! Everyone is up and about from what I can see.

Our coach didn't have a 'proper' sticker on it so we went back to 'Arafāt to pick one up.

We finally arrived in Muzdalifah again and lay out our sleeping gear. We brought a huge drum with us and filled it up with water to make wudhū' with in the morning.

SCENTED TIP

Bring bottles or containers that you can use to make wudhū' with at Fajr time. *Highly necessary!*

Mum was out like a light and I watched her sleep. This was all she had ever asked for. All those years crying thinking she wouldn't get to be here and now

she was fast asleep in Muzdalifah.

Zinger and the gang were out for the count too but I couldn't sleep.

Somehow I nodded off and was awoken by Zinger mightily punching me (how unnecessary) telling me that it was time for Fajr. We did wudhû' and prayed. People started to look for their stones but I had got mine in 'Arafāt which caused a bit of contention. In no time whatsoever, the queues for the coaches became huge.

Uncle thought we should walk but mum wasn't happy with that idea so he set off alone, and planned to meet us in Minā. *Proper soldier.* Our new nickname for him is 'Uncle Dundee' as he can track us down anywhere.

You have to have seen the scenes of chaos and carnage that followed to truly understand. This was my biggest fear on the actual days of Hajj. Nothing else worried me as much as the morning of Muzdalifah.

The queue jumping was shameful. By the time we got out of the compound it was mayhem. People were not going to play fair and were more than willing to harm others to get ahead.

Zinger and the gang decided to wait for the coach but I decided we had no choice but to walk it. Staying here would pose all sorts of fitnah that I didn't want to be subjected to.

I had no idea how, but mum had got an old woman holding her hand. She lost the people she was with and decided to come with us. We had to walk extra slow to accommodate. I was worried as the people we were following were getting further and further away, but I kept finding people I knew from our group for which I was grateful.

Somebody pointed out that a group in front of us with a huge green flag, were in the camp next to us. Turns out they're from my Lovely Luton! I happily became a part of their group for the next hour as we walked to our camp.

We were definitely among the first to make it back. It was a huge relief.

I really have to discuss the concept of travelling light with mum. My hands are aching.

I phoned Zinger who told me that they were not even close to getting on a coach and were going to wait until the end. He told me that there were huge standoffs between groups trying to get on coaches.

SCENTED TIP
Walking may seem difficult but it may be the better option if you can walk long distances.

Uncle decided he wanted to go right away for stoning. We got a small posse together and we were off. It took just over an hour to get to the Jamarāt and the talbiyyah in the tunnels was deafening.

No matter what year you go in, the scene of people walking towards the

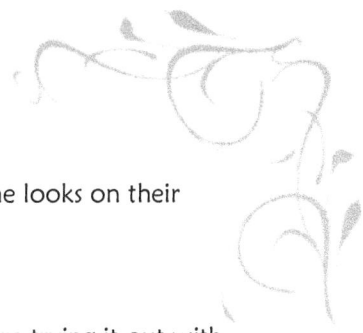

Jamarāt is awesome. You can tell the first timers from the looks on their faces.

In the distance I saw the new train. I heard that they were trying it out with three thousand VIP's on board. Amazing how they can get a train running but cannot sort out the wudhû' facilities in Muzdalifah.

The Jamarāt was easy alhamdulillāh. As always, we managed to get right up close to it.

The walk back took us a bit longer as we took a different route. It was crazy heat but uncle got us back.

There are little things here that you don't usually notice, and it is amazing when you do notice them... Like the ice left in your cup after a drink. Normally you would leave it - but not here. Here, ice is like gold - and can win you many friends.

The meals are very basic but when you're hungry they taste so good. Humans can survive on a lot less. We just choose not to.

You see some tents with mattresses as thick as the ones you have on your beds back home and you think it's such a luxury when all it is, is a mattress.

People come for Hajj but moan when they don't get a five star holiday. Strange.

We finally got confirmation on the Qurbāni, so we snipped a bit of hair to come out of ihrām. It was a great feeling. The comb came out and the beard got dealt with.

Uncle is a huge blessing - he's like my personal 'Bat Signal'. No matter where I am, he finds me. It is such a weight off my mind to know that I won't be stranded here like Crusoe. We called on him to help us find a barber to shave our heads. In the daytime barbers were queuing up to cut hair, but now there was not a single one in sight. Uncle found us two brothers who cut our hair. They did a great job.

A Swansea lad admitted that he was upset with uncle for bringing us back the long way, as he had his little son with him. After talking to some people in our group, he realised that if we had come back the way they went, it would have taken a lot longer than it did. Nice of him to admit that. Uncle the Sat Nav - *committed to finding us the quickest route.*

I had hunger pangs but couldn't find a biryāni seller to save my life. When you don't want something you find tons of it. I had to settle for chips instead.

Moshy, our roomie, owns a shop back home and from the looks of things, he has brought most of the shop with him. Oh the treats we have!

Today was day two of Jamarāt. We went towards them the long way round, but it felt like it only took us about ten minutes. Amazing energy, and amazing barakah in time.

Mum is really in her element here.

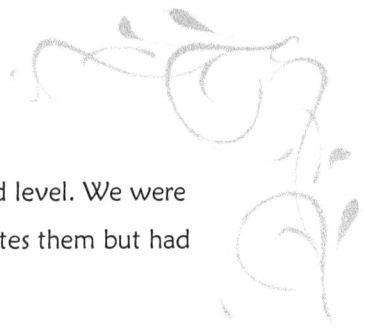

We got to the Jamarāt and decided to go up to the third level. We were quickly faced with mum's biggest fear. Escalators. She hates them but had no choice.

She held my hand and I helped her up all eight of them one after the other. We arrived and with complete ease again we did the stoning and made our way back.

The guards are a lot more organised than past Hajj years, and generally don't allow you to hang around to take photos, or even to go back the way you came.

On the way back we found an old couple who were lost. The woman was in absolute pieces and was literally wailing. I smiled as I watched mum comfort her and take her by the hand. Mum was so calm that she was reassuring others. Another indication to the huge mercy Allāh has bestowed upon us here.

Uncle left me and mum while he took the old couple back to their camp. He came back for us and we were off again. We went a little bit further and found another four people who had been lost since yesterday. Uncle helped them too, and then we finally made our way back to our own camp.

We are really fortunate to have one of the senior UK Imāms in our group. I was always impressed by how he conducted himself on television Q & A programmes, and in person he is even more amazing. May Allāh give me manners like him. We continue to benefit from him greatly throughout our time here.

Muzdalifah

We have a new member in our little group - a brother from Birmingham. He isn't really a new member as I have seen him many, many times on this trip. He had been a coolness to my eyes each time I came across him. So for now, we shall dub him Mr C - a science teacher by profession. A true gentle giant. There are many reasons I love him and one of them is that he's one of the characters who implements what he knows.

The first time we met was at Jeddah Airport and it was him who gave the bottle of water to my mum in the beginning. I will never, ever forget that. It was befitting for that to be our first encounter.

My new nickname is 'Uncle Junior'. I don't get it myself but the lads like it, so who am I to deprive them of their joy?

Zinger wanted to go on an adventure and after haggling with a couple of perfume sellers who line the streets, we found one that we decided we were going to work for, free of charge. We sat on either side of him, and took a shot at it, Apprentice style.

I don't think this bloke had ever sold as much stock as he did today. People were flocking around us, and the great thing about crowds is that they attract bigger crowds. The bloke just could not bag the stuff quick enough. Everyone wanted the bargains we were offering. It doesn't matter about the nationality or the tongue; a laugh and a smile is currency in every country of the world.

Zinger is a blessing in himself. He is firm but very fair. Truly the souls are like conscripted soldiers. There is not much I will not do, but with Zinger by my

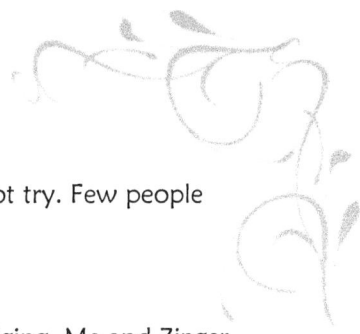

side, I know nothing is safe and there is nothing I will not try. Few people have the effect on me that Zinger has.

By the time business was over, the chap's wallet was bulging. Me and Zinger clocked out for salāh.

Uncle has come up with a plan. He wants us to go to Makkah tonight for tawāf and sa'ī, and come back before Fajr. I think it would make a lot of sense and thankfully mum agreed to it.

After 'Eshā, uncle told us to get ready as rain was coming. Huge winds started the proceedings by blowing away at the tents and the dust got right into our eyes and faces. This was it. I knew it. So many people kept saying that the hard part was over and we were almost home. I kept telling them about 2004 when we had finished and were flooded out. It is not over until Allāh wills it to be over.

I was so worried that we were going to pay for other people's words.

Mother Nature

"It is He Who sends the winds as glad tidings before His Mercy..." (Sûrah al-'Arâf 7: 57)

We started to walk as thunder and lightning prepared to strike above us. I was making non-stop du'â that it would hold, as we were in no man's land with no cover on our heads, and more importantly, mum was with us.

Guards were not letting us cut through the camps. If I wasn't on Hajj they would have been flung out of my way, but patience had got me this far, why would I turn my back on it now? We marched on.

The army was clearing the roads and people were running for cover because of the brewing storm. If it had been any other time, I would have stood there in awe watching the scenes, but not now.

The beggars were *still* out and the amusing thing was, they were carrying on as if nothing was happening. Committed and hard-working people that they are...

Really, truly, mum and I have got to have talk about travelling light soon, as those bags were tearing into my shoulders.

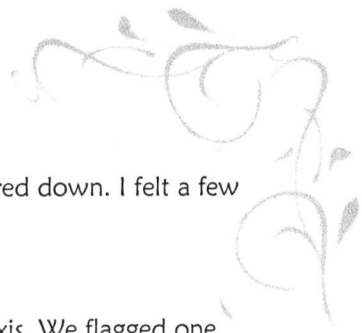

Things were getting tough but the rain still had not poured down. I felt a few heavy drops as an indication of what was on its' way.

We managed to walk back to Makkah and saw some taxis. We flagged one down and subhānallāh, as soon as we got in, rain began to pour down.

Truly, du'ā's are answered in the Sacred Land.

I sat in the car and watched people take shelter in any way that they could. The driver had told us that he was going to charge us around £6 for the journey which got me thinking - the cost of the taxi fare for us was nothing, but how many people were out there in the rain having to brave the wet weather with few clothes on, just because they couldn't afford a simple car journey.

So many things in life we take for granted.

The drive took us about half an hour and it was amazing - all the roads around the Haram were blocked off except for the one we needed to get us right to our hotel. I love these mini miracles.

It felt like weeks since I had seen this place but in reality it had barely been three days. To use a bathroom without queuing behind eight men, power-shower, mattress and peace of mind? *Priceless.*

We had a quick bite to eat and then went to the Haram. It was absolutely empty, and if I didn't have mum with me I would have gone straight for the

Black Stone. It was so empty that we were doing tawāf on the ground floor and I wasn't even holding mum's hand. It was so soul enriching.

We did sa'ī. Feelings of sadness filled me, as this was my last sa'ī before I would be leaving. Some things you wish would never end, and being in the vicinity of the Ka'bah is one of them.

Someone took both mine and uncle's slippers. Mum laughed at us both.

We returned to the hotel and had a kip - early start tomorrow for Minā.

We made our way to Minā before Fajr.

We were keeping busy mingling with people, waiting for the time of Jamarāt to arrive. It was a lot more peaceful and calmer than the last time I was here.

Speaking of last time, we did the Jamarāt and had arranged a meeting point, in case any of our group of around ten people got split up. I got there and found we were three brothers short, so I told everyone else to wait whilst I went to find them. From a distance I spotted the brothers. I thought I could either struggle through the crowd and get them, or I could shout out to them from where I stood. I opted to shout...

It's an awkward feeling when all of a sudden some 40,000 people stop what they are doing and look right at you...

We let the initial crowds go and we made our way. Again, it had been so, so easy. Alhamdulillāh.

The Completion

"Hajj wipes out whatever (sins) came before it." (Muslim)

Our Hajj is officially over and complete.

May Allāh accept it from us, and all those who came to make this blessed journey.

Uncle received and gave big hugs, and mum gave big hugs and lots of kisses.

We started the long trek back to Makkah. There were so many happy faces - beaming with happiness and contentment. In the passageway tunnels there were gangs of motorbike riders who were ferrying people back and forth for a petty price. Obviously time is of the essence so they were going at crazy speeds with passengers hanging off the back.

We made it back and I attempted to have a Radox foot soak but a friend rang to tell me he was outside. I rushed out only to find that he had gone. *Git.* If he wasn't so dear to me I would have jabbed him in his ribs the next time I saw him.

We prayed 'Asr and returned to our room. What happened next was truly amazing.

Rain began to pour down. It poured, and it poured. People ran for cover and lightening flashed. It was unbelievable. Had we not done our tawāf the day before, we would have had to do it now in these conditions. Every single thing has been so smooth, and so perfect.

Allāh is most Just.

The army was blocking the entrances to the Haram but people were forcing their way in. From our hotel window we watched the scenes. I could not see a single bit of ground on the third floor because it was jam packed.

People returned to their hotels *soaked*.

Mum and the ladies wanted tea so I went down to the shopping centre to get some. It was packed out and fights broke out over the lifts. Everyone was going nuts. Why oh why?

Right now, we are worried about Zinger. Everyone in our room is accounted for except for him. A few of us are just watching the scenes from the amazing view I found. Nobody is speaking. Everybody is just transfixed to the view and the scenes.

Tons of umbrellas are going round and round.

For sa'ī, you can see people on the top floor running the whole distance.

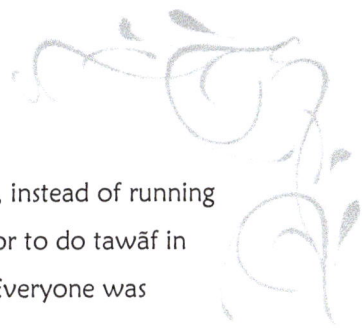

Zinger came back. He told us that when the rain started, instead of running for cover, everyone was trying to get onto the third floor to do tawāf in the rain. He was drenched but smiling from ear to ear. Everyone was shattered so we just rested for a while.

Zinger wanted to sleep at night, yet me and Moshy had other ideas, so we dragged him out with us. We had a good stint in the massage chairs in a mall near out hotel. They proper hit the spot.

While we've been here, we've been making friends with the staff and the security guards. I saw one of the guards reading and asked him what it was. He told me it was *al-Muwatta'* by Imām Mālik ﷺ and then gave it to me as a present. That is brotherhood.

I met up with two amazing brothers today. We sat in my 'amazing-view' location. They tried hard to pretend they weren't impressed, but I knew they were. What felt like a half hour was in fact four hours. Good times.

Today is Friday. I woke up with an aching body this morning. The army seems to have gone and yesterday's scenes of chaos seem to be over.

The army came back two hours before Jummah.

Zinger wanted me to come with him to see a friend of his. The friend brought someone else with him. We showed them the awesome view and then decided we were going to check out the real *big-timers* in Zamzam Towers.

The Completion

We went up around another thirty floors and saw a fire exit. He who
dares, wins - so we took it. We found some stairs and after that, some
more stairs. We twisted and turned until we come out into open air...

We were on the roof of Zamzam Towers.

We were actually ON the ROOF of Zamzam Towers! The green clock was
within throwing distance! The view was out of this world and we couldn't
believe we were really there. Seriously, he who dares, wins.

We prayed up here and were transfixed to the view.

I will never forget that moment. I didn't want to leave with fear of the fact
that I most probably would never find this view again.

We have got to try to find this with the rest of the lads tomorrow.

I was getting some solid sleep until mum woke me up really early. Some of the
ladies gave mum the idea of doing her farewell tawāf at this bizarre time of
morning... We headed to the second floor and mum's energy was amazing.

I was shattered and was really looking forward to getting some sleep between
Dhuhr and 'Asr, but apparently we're going to be moving hotels, even though
we're only here for one more night.

Me and uncle were sorting the luggage out in the corridor and for some
unknown reason it began a chain reaction of everyone thinking they needed to
put their luggage outside as well. Nobody even questioned it.

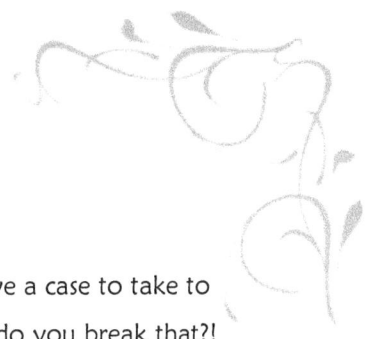

Unquestioning obedience... Scary.

Zinger broke my Radox shower gel handle. Finally I have a case to take to the elder in our room. *Zinger must pay!* How on earth do you break that?!

I forgot to get the case on trial as Zinger bought uncle a big knife to complete the Crocodile Dundee look.

Zinger, Moshy and I went for another chair massage. Moshy's treat - he's a top lad. We tried to muffle the 'ohhhh ahhh' sounds, but it was no good.

We gave Dundee his knife. He loved it.

They moved us to the other hotel for one night. It was a major step down but we have absolutely no right to complain. After the countless blessings bestowed upon us in this journey how could we possibly show any disgust now? Unfortunately not everyone felt the same way.

We dropped our stuff off and decided to go for one last dinner with mum and uncle.

The lads decided that we were going to go for the top-of-the-tower view but the problem was four had now turned to nine, and the security guard was on the prowl after he nabbed Zinger yesterday who by the way, went without me. Turns out he took his wife and not me. The selfish git.

I got a phone call from Terminator our roomie, who wanted in on the action. I went back to look for him, and Swansea lad came with me.

We found him and went again. We walked up nine floors of stairs to avoid the security guard. We twisted and turned and I remembered little markers until **bingo**, we hit the jackpot again. All the lads were there.

We admired the view for a while. A few of them said they would bring their families over the next few days.

We sat outside the hotel eating ice cream and watching the world go by.

Hectic last minute bits and bobs needed sorting out. Mum's new friends all had lists of things that needed doing and getting. No prizes for guessing who got those jobs.

We have gone from a hotel with twelve lifts, to a hotel with one lift, and everyone is trying to get their luggage out at once.

A few of us went out for lunch and ice cream. Again.

I went to the Ka'bah alone.

My last tawāf.
My heart is heavy and it pains.
I don't want to leave you.
I am sorry I haven't spent more time with you.
If only every moment of mine had been spent in gazing at you, taking in every inch, every corner, every bit of you.
My heart sinks.
If only I had more time.

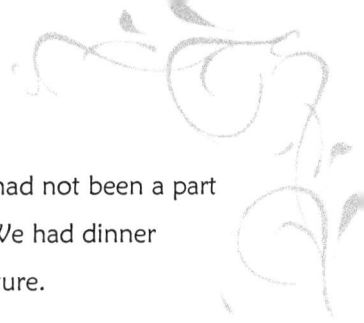

It was also my last night with uncle. For someone who had not been a part of my life for so many years, he was now a huge part. We had dinner together and he gave me some golden advice for my future.

Everyone was fretting over the weight limit, and I bet some serious prayers were being made!

Zinger got us all personalised key-rings, and mine said 'Uncle Jr'. I'm going to miss Zinger's legendary haggling tactics.

We rushed around sorting out last minute stuff and then just chatted away, savouring our final moments in the blessed land of the Messenger of Allah ﷺ, the birthplace of the greatest man on earth. I wondered where his ﷺ home would have been, where the Sahābah ڠ lived, how their daily lives would have been spent here - right here - in the vicinity of the Ka'bah.

I am in awe.

The Goodbye

"By Allāh! You (Makkah) are the most beloved portion of Allāh's earth to me,

and verily you are the most beloved portion of the earth to Allāh too.

Verily you are the best spot on the face of the earth, and the most beloved to Allāh.

If your people did not expel me, I would not have departed from you." (al-Muwatta')

The coaches arrived at 4 a.m. We took our luggage and grabbed our seats.

The second of the two farewells I had been dreading could not be put off for any longer - I had to say goodbye to uncle. That moment will remain in my mind for as long as I live. Never has a goodbye been more emotional for me. Never. Even as I write this it hurts inside.

Coaches tried to move off but it was time for tahajjud. Thousands and thousands of people, as far as the eye could see, filled the roads. They walked with their prayer mats on their shoulders, forsaking their beds to come at this hour to worship. The most beloved place to every single one of them.

It was the most fitting farewell to Makkah I could have wished for. While we moved away back to our homes in England, people were coming in and taking our place. While we watched the human traffic on the roads and the cars that

passed us by, the very people jamming them roads were on their way doing what we were doing just yesterday.

Makkah is never lonely. It is never asleep. It is a dream come true.

We arrived in Jeddah in no time at all. I was a little bit annoyed as to how the luggage was thrown onto the floor and the battle started as we fished for what was ours. There was no order in the queues but we patiently waited for our turn.

Our check-in bloke was not happy and I was seriously worried that he was really going to come down hard on the excess luggage, but it was the complete opposite and he didn't care what we had.

We got the boarding passes and just when I thought this had been the most surreal and blessed Hajj ever... Guess who got business class?

The Conclusion

"The accepted Hajj has no reward but Paradise." (Bukhāri)

Hajj is like a fingerprint. In other words, each one is unique. People say it, but you have to live through the experience to understand it.

Tomorrow we will go back to our lives and forget the valuable lessons we learnt in the time we spent here. Perhaps that was one of the reasons I kept this diary, and would recommend others to do the same.

I will never be grateful enough for the manner in which Allāh blessed us with great accommodation and so many privileges. Given a choice, I would love to come back and live like an average person here, which is more enriching than those who live in the tall high rise towers and enjoy all the perks that come with them. There is beauty in simplicity.

If you want to know yourself better, then mix with the people - see what you learn and be amazed at what you will take away.

Once 'Abdullāh ibn Mas'ūd ﷺ was in a place where nobody knew who he was. When he went to get water from the well, he was pushed and shoved by

the people, but he was still happy, as he got to live as a simple soul.

I will never be able to even stand in his shadow, but maybe I understand a little of what he felt, because every time you leave the hotel there is an adventure to be had - regardless of your background and where you come from.

A smile can open many doors and is understood and welcomed by every single person in this world. To turn your prayer mat sideways and share with the person next to you can make all the difference. Just try it.

I would love to come alone without needing to worry about being responsible for someone, so that I can really push myself to all limits and take maximum benefit from such a place. I'd recommend that whoever has the opportunity to do such a thing, does it now.

"Hasten to do Hajj, for none of you knows what may happen to him." (Ahmad)

I never, ever dreamed I would be here again, and maybe in the future my many nieces will need me as a mahram to bring them. I look forward to it already. Whatever happens - I just cannot get enough of it.

"Keep on doing Hajj and 'Umrah, for they eliminate poverty and sin just as the bellows eliminate impurities from iron, gold and silver." (Tirmidhi)

You will learn so much about yourself. You will learn so much about others. You will be tested in ways you couldn't even imagine.

If you think you have patience, you will find out if you truly do, on Hajj.
If you think you love for others what you love for yourself, you will find out if you truly do, on Hajj.
If you think you can cope in challenging situations, you will find out if you truly can, on Hajj.

A real test is when you are broken, tired, and hungry - and you've just found some shade - but then someone more needy comes along.

A real test is when you have swollen feet, your bed is singing your name, and an elderly couple come and ask you to help them complete tawāf and sa'ī.

A real test is when you find refreshing cold water, but your brothers need it as much as you do, and you have to share.

A real test is when you sit in one place all night trying to keep a good spot for Fajr, and someone comes at the last minute and tries to sit in it with you.

You will appreciate so much more when you are here; your health, when you see the condition of some people during tawāf, yet they keep going, determined; your wealth, when you see that a man's dinner depends on your leftovers, or that a sister cannot eat what she wants, because she's a riyāl short.

Many times in life we are comfortable in our worship and measure ourselves by those who do less than us. Many times in life we see those who have more

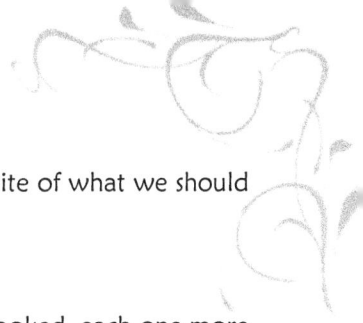

than us and we are not content. It's the complete opposite of what we should be. Being here really redresses that balance.

I saw hundreds and thousands of people everywhere I looked, each one more determined than me to seek the pleasure of Allāh. When measured against these giants, I fell very short and knew I would really have to pick up my game to keep up.

I saw many, many people with a fraction of what I have, but you cannot put a price on the contentment on their faces.

There were so many people, so little crowd control, but on hearing just one voice, the adhān, they would automatically form straight lines and move in unison. Standing together, bowing together, prostrating together. All hungry for the same thing. All yearning for the pleasure of the One who deserves to be worshipped alone.

With regards to my personal journey, in the end I realised a simple, fundamental thing:

After all the worry and stress before and during this journey, there really was no need.

My mother and I truly were Allāh's guests, and Allāh alone looked after us.